YOUR KNOWLEDGE HAS VALUE

AF130180

- We will publish your bachelor's and
  master's thesis, essays and papers

- Your own eBook and book -
  sold worldwide in all relevant shops

- Earn money with each sale

Upload your text at www.GRIN.com
and publish for free

Bibliographic information published by the German National Library:

The German National Library lists this publication in the National Bibliography; detailed bibliographic data are available on the Internet at http://dnb.dnb.de .

This book is copyright material and must not be copied, reproduced, transferred, distributed, leased, licensed or publicly performed or used in any way except as specifically permitted in writing by the publishers, as allowed under the terms and conditions under which it was purchased or as strictly permitted by applicable copyright law. Any unauthorized distribution or use of this text may be a direct infringement of the author s and publisher s rights and those responsible may be liable in law accordingly.

Imprint:

Copyright © 2017 GRIN Verlag
Print and binding: Books on Demand GmbH, Norderstedt Germany
ISBN: 9783668717503

This book at GRIN:

https://www.grin.com/document/426991

Derek McCloskey

Managing Security in Retail Offline and Online

GRIN Verlag

GRIN - Your knowledge has value

Since its foundation in 1998, GRIN has specialized in publishing academic texts by students, college teachers and other academics as e-book and printed book. The website www.grin.com is an ideal platform for presenting term papers, final papers, scientific essays, dissertations and specialist books.

Visit us on the internet:

http://www.grin.com/

http://www.facebook.com/grincom

http://www.twitter.com/grin_com

Managing Security

Derek McCloskey
DT345

Contents

Part – A – Managing Security Offline

Introduction

Shrinkage and retail crime are major issues for retailers, having significant impact on net profitability of stores, products and retail businesses alike. Only a small minority of crimes against the retailer are detected or witnessed at the time or later: the value of losses a retailer faces over a period is normally calculated as shrinkage (or loss of inventory). Within this calculated figure is the inclusion of losses not criminally related such as wastage, pricing errors, and a range of identification and accounting errors and only represents an indirect theft measure. Crime losses from burglary, robbery, and major frauds are not usually included in the shrinkage estimate. (Bamfield, 2004)

Although shrinkage being a major cost to retail, it has received very little academic research or discussion. This is due in part to the inconsistencies in approach by different countries and companies and an unwillingness to share sensitive information, making it difficult to compare and analyse output.

For the purpose of this report, the focus will be on a segment of Musgrave operated stores (MOPI), mainly located in the greater Dublin area. This comprises of 22 stores, making it is possible to plot trends between them all and gauge comparisons under different criteria.

Part A reflects on offline managing security in the bricks and mortar environment firstly this report will look at how shrinkage is calculated how it is measured on a global scale and how that measures against the name group of stores. It will then go into the named company's policies and procedures and highlight improvements that can be made and strengths that already exist. After reflecting on some useful technology solutions, it will close out Part A by offering recommendations and conclusion.

Part B of this report will look more at combating security on the online environment, by firstly reviewing the types of threats faced B2C e-commerce companies, secondly understanding what a fully integrated protection system is. Finally it will look at the balance of trust, loyalty and security and provide a conclusion on security online.

Method Employed when calculating Shrinkage

The method employed within the MOPI stores is the same generally used across much of the retail industry. This involves the physical counting of stock four times a year (quarterly) and the result of that count being applied to a formula to calculate loss. The formula applied when calculating stock loss is:

Retail Shrink = Optimal Retail Value or Income – Actual Retail Value or Income

This gives MOPI the value in monetary terms, but the company evaluates performance based on the percentage of overall sale's; this is further calculated to be:

Total Losses / Total Sales = Retail Shrink %

MOPI uses this percentage figure to compare stores within the group against each other, regardless of turnover and put stores into peer groups.

Areas of high importance are counted more regularly such as high value products and fresh departments. Fresh departments are counted on a bi-weekly basis and reported on through margins for analysis. The reason for this is that they can be tracked closer and intervention can be taken when an issue arises to minimise loss. High value items, also known as hot products, are generally high value, highly desirable, easily concealable and easy to sell on, are also counted bi-weekly. (Clarke, 1999)

Understanding how to calculate shrinkage in retail is important, understanding how to impact and control these results is even more important as it can impact company profitability. Controlling retail shrinkage is one of the key aspects of being a successful retailer.

Brittain states that, shrinkage is a much more complicated problem than simply accounting for the theft of merchandise and the direct loss of profit, its about inventory control, which involves the management of the supply, accessibility, storage, and delivery of the company's goods. As a result, shrink management strategies require a multifaceted approach in order to successfully manage the process. This is an important concept for every retail manager to learn and understand and will have a direct impact on the company — and individual store – performance. (Brittain, 2017)

The Global Retail Theft Barometer

The Global Retail Theft Barometer is the first and only global research on the cost of shrink, comprised of shoplifting, employee or supplier fraud and administrative errors. The study, launched originally in 2001 in Europe by retailer's. Demand was expanded in 2008 to Asia and the Americas, providing data to help retailers around the world benchmark their performance against averages for specific category groups, markets and geographies. This research was conducted by Ernie Deyle; a leading expert in retail loss prevention: and 'The Smart Cube'; a global professional services firm that specialises in custom research and analytics services to corporations, financial services and management consulting firms globally. The report itself was commissioned by Checkpoint Services (Checkpoint S. , 2015).

The last time that Ireland was part of the survey was 2010 when the Global Retail Theft Barometer indicated that the global economic recession was a major contributor to a world-wide spike in shrink rates. The 2010 survey had 1,103 respondents from retail providing information relating to shrink, relevant to the period from July 2009 until June 2010. This is widely believed to be when many regional economies stabilized and resumed growth after the economic collapse. A key finding of the report is that Global shrink was at $107.3 billion (US) or 1.36% of global retail sales. Ireland in this report had a shrink percentage of 1.32 making it 0.4% below the global average. In the 2015 report shrinkage had fallen to 1.23% for global sales although Ireland was not represented in this survey. (Deyle, 2015)

MOPI v's International Comparison

As Ireland was not part of the 2015 research, we will compare the results in MOPI to the shrink average in the UK for this period. Note that this is a general comparison as the research dates are from July 2014 – June 2015 and the MOPI results are 2015, also the UK is taken as our most comparable neighbor as our economies are very intertwined, although the scale of the UK market is much larger and would perhaps provide lower % in terms. In this instance the UK's shrinkage as a percentage of sales was 0.89% but if this is broken down further to supermarket and grocery retailers as a category this comes in at 1.01% of sales. (Checkpoint, 2015) MOPI's shrinkage for a similar period was 1.15%. Both are below the global average of 1.23%. Since 2015 however, MOPI shrink has improved considerably with a 2016 company average of 0.98% and the current year to date (YTD) running at 0.64%. There have been numerous internal work-streams formed to work on this improvement which will be discussed further on.

The research from 2015, highlights in the UK that within food retail the hot products most susceptible to shrinkage are beers/wine/spirits (BWS), cheese, and fresh meat and within the health and beauty element of the store razor blades and creams. (Checkpoint, 2015) In relation to MOPI these categories would be similar problem categories with the exception of cheese. BWS would be average at 1.5% YTD down from 1.75% in 2015; Meat is 1.0% YTD down from 1.4% in 2015. Two other problem categories within MOPI are Baby which has been consistently high at 1.9% since 2015; and Bread/Cakes at 1.25% YTD which is down from a high of 4.2% in 2015.

Sources of Shrinkage

In relation to the global perspective 2015 the barometer report breaks shrinkage out into four categories of sources. It cites dishonest employee theft to be the highest factor at 39%; followed by shop lifting at 38%; admin/non-crime loss at 16%; and supplier fraud 7%. This conflicts with the UK part of the report which illustrates that admin and non-crime loss accounts for 40% of the loss. It further illustrates that shoplifting accounts for 26%; employee theft 25% and supplier fraud at 10%. (Checkpoint, 2015) The sources outlined in the 2015 barometer report mirror the categories discussed by Chapman under categories of shrinkage, which are outlined as process failures, internal theft, external theft and inter-company fraud. (Chapman, 2006)

The improvements that have been made across the MOPI business in the last 3 years can mainly been accredited to the improvement made in the administration/non-crime loss aspect of the business. A good example of this can been seen in the bread/cake shrinkage which improved from 4.2% to 1.25%. This has been through the standardization of the product being sold. MOPI operates a scratch bakery in approximately 85% of the stores, it was found that not all stores where following the correct product information set out in the guides (PIG). A scone that was being sold in one store was twice the size of a scone being sold in another. A work-stream was initiated centrally to visit all stores and revisit the guides and make improvements to standardize range, this included in some cases the commissioning of new plant or equipment which was fit for purpose to achieve correct weights and measures. A further intervention was to slice, bag and tag all in-store produced products to ensure it went through the checkouts under the correct label.

Other aspects of improvement in this source was better administration in terms of logging paperwork/dockets and returns processes and has led to product being accounted for correctly.

MOPI Policy and Procedures

MOPI doesn't necessarily have an outlined security policy but a number of procedures that are followed and audited upon. These include cash office audits; key control logs; daily security checklist; arrest and recovery records; colleague check records; security lockdown checklists; intruder alarm logs and checks; and building security checklist. These procedures are audited on a quarterly basis by a member of the central operations team.

This audit also captures other aspects of the processes including staff awareness and communication and training. The problem with this is the lack of consistency around afore mentioned checklists and logs. Whilst they must be carried out, on occasion something else takes precedent, and the checklist will take a backseat for a period. Also, the number of colleagues that are specialized on the complete process is very few and can make is difficult to maintain the process end to end.

Staff Awareness, Communication and Training

Firstly, hiring the right colleague can reduce shrink by 13%. Things like background checks, previous employment verification, and written integrity surveys help ensure a more honest employee. (Park City Group) In some cases, at store level these checks are not thorough enough.

Once a colleague is on-board, an important pillar of ensuring awareness around shrink is good communication. As set out by Quirke 1996, the internal communicator should be trying to link communication to what is at the top of their agenda. In order to create awareness and understanding at a shop floor level, communications need to be clear, simple to understand and quantify relatively to the colleague. (Quirke, 1996) This is done in MOPI through a shrink communications board accompanied by shrink huddles instore. The communications board will hold the usual information such as value of shrink, percentage, and breakdown of information by departments. In order to make colleagues understand the value of missing stock it is quantified on the communication board as simply the number of baskets of shopping leaving the store for free. Example, if a store has a quarterly loss of ten thousand euro and an average basket of fifteen euro this is displayed as 667 baskets leaving the store unaccounted for. The huddles bring light to daily issues that can be affected to improve results. It is also a means of creating awareness amongst colleagues of the who, what and when and in many cases colleagues can themselves highlight and communicate back any issues they have seen themselves. Again, the main downside to this is having huddles on a consistent basis or reaching every colleague in the store due to operating times or colleague rostering. The main focus is on educating the key colleagues and this has a trickle-down effect. This is quite strong within the MOPI stores.

Training is extremely powerful and cost-effective investment by any organization, but only if it is implemented to match and compliment the needs of the business. (Denby, 2010) In MOPI this training is geared towards colleagues understanding the processes in their own area of the store, to achieve results by individual departments, when a colleague receives on the job training on how to process waste or transfers they build up the skills set and then graduate on to more complicated processes such as transfers etc. This is developed through experience first in one department and then they may move to another department were although most of the processes are the same it's some of the principles that are different. One thing that colleagues probably don't get, is a fuller understanding of what the implications are for not following procedures correctly. This could be something that is explored further.

Technology

Smart Displays

Smart display systems, although currently used mainly in electronic goods stores, are a useful tool that help prevent stock loss. This would be very adaptable for food retailers and could primarily be focused on hot products. This would help lower the exposure for retailers by minimizing the stock loss to one or two items at a time. There are many live examples in the industry were perpetrators clear shelves of high value goods and are gone in a matter of minutes. This technology allows for high theft products to be displayed openly rather than locked up. If several items are taken from a display, the smart system triggers an alarm or a signal to a loss prevention person who may be able to stop thieves before they leave the store. (Gregory, 2013)

Radio Technology Identification (RFID's)

RFID's come in the form of chips embedded in product tags or packages. These chips contain product information and enable retailers to track items using their stock control system, so merchants can gain real-time inventory visibility and accuracy. (Nicasio, 2017) The technology can also help retailers catch shoplifters. If someone attempts to walk out of the shop with RFID tags still attached to the merchandise, your store's security sensors could go off and alert your staff. Within MOPI this technology has been rolled in a small number of stores as a trial. This works by the store being able to attach small metal tags to products and this will alarm if it passes an antenna without first going through the correct checkout procedure that will disarm the tag. An example of this being applied live in the store, is if a customer requests a large amount of fillet steak at the butchers counter, and the butcher is suspicious, they can attach a discreet tag unknown to the customer. If this passes the proper checkout process the customer is none the wiser but if the product doesn't an alarm will go off, then the customer can be apprehended. This has sometimes failed to deactivate and could lead to an embarrassing stoppage but if the stoppage is dealt with by the security in the correct manner there is generally no issue.

Recommendations and Conclusion

With regard too calculating shrinkage within MOPI there is quite a robust system in place. The skills and understanding of those involved in the process has also improved greatly this has taken time due to the change over from Superquinn to SuperValu and the Musgrave ways of working. This was done through hothousing poor departments such as bread and cakes and working a s team to find solutions and best practices. In recent times these sessions have ceased, and a recommendation of this report would be to bring these back in some form as a means of continuous improvement.

In relation audits that are carried out these are measured and are way of help management teams understand where weaknesses are but there is very little follow through unless stores have a serious shrinkage issue. More onus needs to be put on the follow through as a means of improving results further and creating more specialist at store level.

Staff awareness, communication and training is relatively strong around shrinkage in most stores, especially amongst the core team in most stores this is due to it being a live environment and its sometimes easy to spot those offenders whilst they are in the store. If someone is stopped for shop lifting, colleagues can see what's going and act as good eyes and ears around the store. The key point for improvement here would be to get the evening and weekend colleagues tuned into the same mantra.

The point of view of the company has changed, instead of looking at stock loss it looks at the profitability number of the store. Stores are always going to have shrink but the view is now how do we as managers offset that loss. This can be done through several streams; one is better buying of promotional stock exiting promotions and selling it for the full retail; another is doing deals with suppliers for free stock if certain case quantities are met.

All of the practices and procedures set out in this report all go together to help reduce shrink and each is as important as each other. The success of anti-shrink initiatives lies just not in the tools, but how they are used and implemented at store level.

Part B – Managing Security On-Line

Introduction

Information technology (IT) has played an important role in affecting the scale and nature of retailing. (Reynolds, 2000) As traditional commerce and e-commerce merge, so too do the threats. With 70% of the Irish population using the internet every day for various functions the possibility of stolen information is extremely high. (TNS Opinin and Social, 2015) Non-ecommerce companies also have information that needs protection. There is a vast amounts of information held about customers, by businesses, on computers around the world. Any attack can be detrimental to the company involved through loss of information and reputation. Therefore, security is a must. To achieve the highest level of security and protect data requires the development and implementation of new technologies, the organization to implement policies and procedures which meet industry standards and government laws. There are various types of cyber-attacks with various objectives although primarily its is to a) steal data or, b) disrupt services.

There are two perspectives on ecommerce security, that of business and the other of the consumer. These can be measured across a number of dimensions including confidentiality, access control, integrity, availability and authenticity. There are tensions that exist between security and other values. The ease of use can be affected the more security features that are added to sites making them slower, public safety is also an issue as criminals are increasingly using technology to plan crimes or threaten states. (Chahar, 2013)

The Threats Facing the B2C E-Commerce Company

As you can access the internet on almost everything these days, the number of vulnerabilities are increasing all the time. There are three key points of vulnerability: the client; the server; and the communications pipeline.

For this report we will review five examples of the most common security threats experienced by business to customer ecommerce.

Denial of Service (DOS)

A denial-of-service attack is a security event that occurs when an attacker takes action that prevents legitimate users from accessing targeted computer systems, devices or other network resources. (TechTarget, 2017)

Denial-of-service (DoS) attacks typically flood servers, systems or networks with traffic to overwhelm the victim resources and make it difficult or impossible for legitimate users to use them. From an online retailer's perspective this is a huge problem. Large retailers now use mirror systems; where by they can take down systems and replace them with exact replica.

Ransomeware

This is a threat that has become more prevalent this year. Ransomware is a type of malware that prevents you from using your computer or accessing certain files unless you pay a ransom. It often encrypts files so that they cannot be opened. Examples of ransomware include Reveton, CryptoLocker, and CryptoWall. (TechTerms , 2017) Ransomware is often distributed as a trojan, or malware disguised as a legitimate file. Once installed, it may lock your computer and display a "lockscreen" with a message saying you must pay a ransom to regain use of your computer. A number of high profile companies have been affected by this threat including Musgraves. The best way to deal with ransomware is to prevent it, by having sufficient antivirus and updating with any new patches that are released.

Viruses

A computer virus is a program or piece of code that is loaded onto your computer without your knowledge and runs against your wishes. Viruses can also replicate themselves. All computer viruses are man-made. A simple virus that can make a copy of itself over and over again, and is relatively easy to produce. Even such a simple virus can be dangerous because it will quickly use all available memory and bring the system to a halt. An even more dangerous type of virus is one capable of transmitting itself across networks and bypassing security systems. (Norton, n.d.) there are many antivirus programs to choose from.

Worms

A computer worm is a type of malicious software program whose primary function is to infect other computers while remaining active on infected systems. A computer worm is self-replicating malware that duplicates itself to spread to uninfected computers. Worms often use parts of an operating system that are automatic and invisible to the user. It is common for worms to be noticed only when their uncontrolled replication consumes system resources, slowing or halting other tasks. (TechTarget, 2017) An important distinction between computer viruses and worms is that viruses require an active host program or an already-infected and active operating system in order to run, cause damage and infect other executable files or documents, while worms are stand-alone malicious programs that can self-replicate.

Bots and Botnets

Bots and botnets are a growing threat and continue to be one of the most sophisticated and popular types of cybercrime. Your computer can become infected without your knowledge and through simple methods such as spam emails with attachments. Once the spam attachment is opened, the virus will be activated, and the computer will be infected.

Bots can also be used online to carry out repetitive processes such as buying up concert tickets. So, websites have screening questions that must be answered by a live user as a means of combatting this.

With so many threats online, it is important to have the correct protection against these in order to protect data and maintain the trust of the public.

Fully Integrated Protection Systems

There are many available on the market from many different companies but for the purpose of this report we will look at firewalls in general and how they operate.

Firewalls

In computing, a firewall acts as a barrier between a trusted system or network and outside connections, such as the Internet. However, a computer firewall is more of a filter than a wall, allowing trusted data to flow through it. A firewall can be created using either hardware or software. (TechTarget, 2014) Many businesses and organizations protect their internal networks using hardware firewalls. A single or double firewall may be used to create a demilitarized zone (DMZ), which prevents untrusted data from ever reaching the LAN (local area network). Software firewalls are more common for individual users and can be custom configured via a software interface. Windows operating systems on your home PC often has its own firewall built in, but more advanced firewall utilities can be installed with Internet security software.

See image below of how a firewall works:

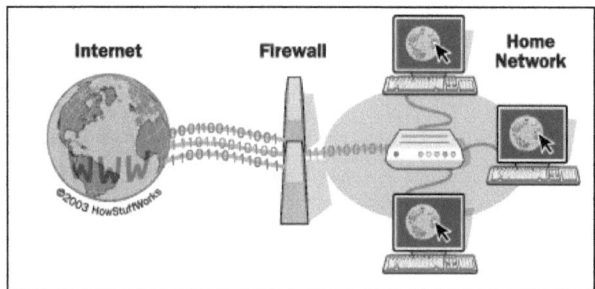

(Unknown)

In relation to how firewalls protect and work for businesses, large corporations often have very complex firewalls in place to protect their extensive networks. On the outbound side, firewalls can be configured to prevent employees from sending certain types of emails or transmitting sensitive data outside of the network. On the inbound side, firewalls can be programmed to prevent access to certain websites (like social networking sites). Additionally, firewalls can prevent outside computers from accessing computers inside the network. A company might choose to designate a single computer on the network for file sharing and all other computers could be restricted. There is no limit to the variety of configurations that are possible when using firewalls. Extensive configurations typically need to be handled and maintained by highly trained IT specialists.

Firewalls can't protect malicious users from gaining access to the internal systems if someone has given them the required passwords. Firewalls are also only as secure as the system they are operating on. It is important to properly secure the entire system. It will not protect businesses if the system in which it is protecting isn't secure, it needs to work as part of an overall security architecture. (Welch-Albernathy, 2004)

The main over riding factor between B2C e-commerce is the need for trust, trust that they are protected if using a businesses website to disclose personal data.

The Balance of Trust, Loyalty and Security

Two factors that have a contribution to the success, and contribute to loyalty, of e-businesses are the trust consumers place in the online business and how secure they feel when they use the businesses platforms. Trust in the offline sense is built up between the interaction between two people, but online there is none of this and trust relies heavily on brand names and reliable sources. Trust on the online sense is the consumers trust's that the merchant will deliver the product or service paid for within a reasonable time and with an acceptable level of customer service. (Srinivason, 2004)

Building Trust

In an environment deprived of face-to-face human contact, there are huge gains for the businesses that know how to build customer trust online. This report reviews some of the mechanisms used to build trust online.

Being Transparent

This is about being open to your customers. Understand how you can simply answer questions and inform them of processes. A good aspect in this is frequently asked questions section on the site, this would cover information about ordering etc. It is also beneficial to answer questions about yourself such as codes of ethics.

Publicize Failures

If something has gone wrong, it is important to let people know there is something wrong and this will only help to build loyalty. Everyone makes mistakes, what makes the difference is how mistakes are dealt with.

Be Likeable and Humanize

Companies commonly express their values through mission statements and this is what helps customers relate to what the company is trying to achieve. This can be done in different ways and helps build up a picture in the consumers mind of the sort of business they are dealing with.

Get External Proof

If a site or an online company has had a good review or has been endorsed by a reputable source, it will publicize this on their site as a means proof that they are trustworthy as a business.

These are a few of the tactics used by online companies. At this stage the customers trust has been gained and they decide to give over their personal details the onus is now on the merchant to provide the security. (Sven, 2016)

Security

As discussed there are many ways to build trust, but it is important to secure transaction online as this is essentially the leap of faith that the customer is taking. This is done through transacting across what is known as an SSL (Secure Socket Layers). SSL is the standard security technology for establishing an encrypted link between a web server and a browser. This link ensures that all data passed between the web server and browsers remain private and integral. SSL is an industry standard and is used by millions of websites in the protection of their online transactions with their customers. Other methods of providing online security are digital certificates and SET (secure electronic transactions) both are based around encryption protocols.

Conclusion

Trust is clear factor that contributes to the success of e-commerce. It is the result of building together a number of elements of reputation, technology and encouraging a relationship with the end user. This is like retailing in bricks and mortar environment in terms of building customer relationships.

There are any number of constant threats from cyber crime and this will always be evolving, and companies must always be aware of the threats and the dangers they can pose in terms of destroying that customer relationship.

References

Bamfield, J. (2004). Shrinkage, shoplifting and the cost of retail crime in Europe: a cross sectional analysis of major retailers in 16 European countries. *International Journal of Retail Management, 32*(5), pp. 235-241.

Brittain, J. (2017, May 11). *How to Calculate Shrinkage in Retail*. Retrieved from losspreventionmedia.com: http://losspreventionmedia.com/insider/inventory-shrinkage/how-to-calculate-shrinkage-in-retail/

Chahar, D. (2013). The Study of E-Commerce Security Issues and Solutions. *International Journal of Advanced research in computer and communicatyion engineering*, pp. 2885-2892. Retrieved from https://s3.amazonaws.com/academia.edu.documents/34107189/69-o-Niranjanamurthy_-The_study_of_E-Commerce_Security_Issues_and_Solutions.pdf?AWSAccessKeyId=AKIAIWOWYYGZ2Y53UL3A&Expires=1513204993&Signature=ZdAw6Yd9Nct2%2FdsNnBA8ruUns8w%3D&response-content-dis

Chapman, P. (2006). Methods for Measuring Shrinkage. *Security Journal, 19*(4), pp. 228-240.

Checkpoint. (2015, Nov 3rd). Global Retail Theft Barometer Trade Report UK 2015. YouTube.com. Retrieved from https://www.youtube.com/watch?v=R4OLL_gtNO8

Checkpoint, S. (2015). *About the Global Retail Theft Barometer*. Retrieved from The Global Retail Theft Barometer: http://www.globalretailtheftbarometer.com/index.html#about

Clarke, R. (1999). *Hot Products: Understanding, Anticipating and Reducing the Demand for Stolen Goods*. London: HMSO. Retrieved from http://citeseerx.ist.psu.edu/viewdoc/download?doi=10.1.1.424.3416&rep=rep1&type=pdf

Denby, S. (2010). The importance of training needs anaylsis. *Industrial and Commercial Training, 42*(3), pp. 147-150.

Deyle, E. (2015). *The Global Retail theft Barometer 2014-2015*. Checkpoint.

Gregory, J. (2013, November 7th). *3 Ways Tech is Stopping Theft*. Retrieved from entrepreneur.com: https://www.entrepreneur.com/article/229674

Nicasio, F. (2017, September 12). *Retail Loss Prevention: 7 Powerful Tools and Technologies to Help Reduce Shrinkage.* Retrieved from VendBlog: https://blog.vendhq.com/post/64901828723/loss-prevention-retail-6-powerful-tools-technologies-help-reduce-shrinkage

Norton. (n.d.). *What is a computer virus?* Retrieved from Norton.com: https://us.norton.com/internetsecurity-malware-what-is-a-computer-virus.html

Park City Group. (n.d.). *Shrinking Shrink: Best Practices for Managing Shrink.* Park City: Park City Group. Retrieved from https://www.parkcitygroup.com/wp-content/uploads/WP_Shrinking_Shrink_04032012.pdf

Quirke, B. (1996). Putting communication on the managements agenda. *Journal of communication management, 1*(1), pp. 67-79.

Reynolds, J. (2000). eCommerce: A Critical Review. *International Journal of Retail and Distribution Management, 28*(10), pp. 417-444.

Srinivason, S. (2004). Role of Trust in E-Business Success. *Information Management and Computer Security*, pp. 66-72.

Sven. (2016, April 21). *8 Ways to Build Customer Trust in E-Commerce.* Retrieved from Userlike.com: https://www.userlike.com/en/blog/build-customer-trust-ecommerce

TechTarget. (2014, November 21). *Firewall.* Retrieved from TechTarget.com: http://searchsecurity.techtarget.com/definition/firewall

TechTarget. (2017). *Denial-of-service attack.* Retrieved from TechTarget: http://searchsecurity.techtarget.com/definition/denial-of-service

TechTerms . (2017, April 21). *Ransomeware.* Retrieved from techterms.com: https://techterms.com/definition/ransomware

TNS Opinin and Social. (2015). *Cyber Security Report.* European Commision - Director General for Communication. Retrieved from http://ec.europa.eu/commfrontoffice/publicopinion/archives/ebs/ebs_423_en.pdf

Unknown. (n.d.). *How a firewall works?* Retrieved from https://www.google.ie/search?q=images+of+firewalls&tbm=isch&tbo=u&source=uni

v&sa=X&ved=0ahUKEwiEstWyqIrYAhWJAxoKHV8rDxMQsAQIKA&biw=1607
&bih=727#imgrc=l5vWjI_aEync5M:

Welch-Albernathy, D. (2004, September 3). *Introduction to Firewalls*. Retrieved from InformIT.com: http://www.informit.com/articles/article.aspx?p=170452&seqNum=2

YOUR KNOWLEDGE HAS VALUE

- We will publish your bachelor's and
  master's thesis, essays and papers

- Your own eBook and book -
  sold worldwide in all relevant shops

- Earn money with each sale

Upload your text at www.GRIN.com
and publish for free